# Chloe's Destiny

Written and Illustrated by

Bridget Smith

Copyright 2008 by Bridget Smith.

All rights reserved. No part of this book may be reproduced or transmitted in any form by any means, electronic or mechanical, including photocopying, recording, or by any information storage and retrieval system without permission in writing from the copyright owner.

This is a work of fiction. Names, characters, places and incidents either are the product of the author's imagination or are fictitiously, and any resemblance to any actual persons, living or dead, events, or locales is entirely coincidental

To order additional copies of this book, visit
bridgetbuildscharacter.com

# DEDICATION

Dedicated to my Lord and Savior Jesus Christ. To my loving husband, Sherman Smith, and our children, Jonathan, Blake, and Emilee, who are charming, witty, kind, and who continually enrich our lives

# ACKNOWLEDGEMENTS

**JANE CLAWSON**, an exceptional teacher and librarian, for her encouragement and mentoring which helped to get "it all together"

**LISA MCELROY**, a seasoned and loving educator, who is an inspiration in day to day inquiries in reading strategies.

To my wonderful parents, **EMMITT AND ANN BARNES** who through love and support, gave me the knowledge to seek, to know and to learn from every moment and experience and who gave me a wonderful childhood that centered Jesus Christ.

To one of my favorite teachers, Pam Mathis, who through kindness, intelligences and excitement made science so interesting.

To all my family and friends who have encouraged me in their reading of my story

Special thanks to Kristen Henderson for making my book my own

## ALSO INCLUDED:
Glossary
Comprehensive Questions
Song "Metamorphosis" music composed/lyrics written by Bridget Smith
Illustrations/literature/music by
Bridget Smith

## SUMMARY
Chloe is a caterpillar who finds out what her destiny is as she goes through the stages of metamorphosis. This simple story invites the reader to experience the process of metamorphosis through the eyes of a caterpillar.

Chloe was a beautiful caterpillar.
She crawled everywhere;
on the grass, over the hills, up the trees, and down again.

She frequently noticed the soft, fluffy white clouds, the golden serene sunsets, and the beautiful butterflies fluttering from flower to flower.

She felt it was her destiny to fly, but she didn't know why.

Everyday she would crawl up a tree
to see what it would be like
if she could fly.

Then one day she felt that
she should stay
on one special little branch.
Something inside of her
caused her
to begin making a silky mat,
to which she hung on with her legs.

After shedding

her skin

for one

last time,

she later
revealed
a beautiful
jade green
chrysalis,
which is a hardening
of the caterpillar's
skin.

Then she fell fast asleep. While she was in the pupa stage of her life,

she felt her body was changing.

Finally,
after many days,
her body
had completely changed.

She felt the strength
of her wings
as the hemolymph
pumped through her body.

As she
was flying around,
she saw
her reflection in the water.
She had
the most beautiful colors
she had ever seen.
Then,
she realized
why she had always
wanted to fly.

This is her destiny
and now her destiny
had been fulfilled.
She could now
tell other caterpillars
they to have a destiny.
Each caterpillar is special
in his or her own way.
One day, all caterpillars
will become what
they were intended to be.

# GLOSSARY

**CHRYSALIS**- the chrysalis is a hardened shell where the insect will grow and change. This change during the middle of the life cycle of insects is called the pupa stage.

**Destiny**- events that will automatically happen to a specific person or thing in the future.

**HEMOLYMPH**- a fluid, which is pumped into the wing veins, consist of proteins and other nutrients to help support the exoskeleton of the insect.

**METAMORPHOSIS**- an abrupt physical change; chaining from one shape into another. This usually happens in distinct stages, starting with the embryo, then the larva (caterpillar) or nymph, going through the pupa stage, and ending as an adult (butterfly).

Check out the other books in the
# CONCEPT AND CHARACTER SERIES

Chloe's Destiny

If I could count to ten...

What About Me?

Made in the USA
Middletown, DE
03 February 2022